GW01057401

Original title:
Heartfelt Murmurs

Editor: Jessica Elisabeth Luik
Author: Aurelia Lende
ISBN HARDBACK: 978-9916-86-188-2
ISBN PAPERBACK: 978-9916-86-189-9

Quiet Confessions

In the hush of twilight's glow,
Whispers of secrets softly flow.
Beneath the stars, our stories weave,
In silent vows, we do believe.

Moonlight dances on the floor,
Unspoken dreams we both implore.
Eyes that speak and lips that smile,
Sharing hearts in quiet style.

Night's embrace gently surrounds,
Where love in silence truly abounds.
In every breath, a promise kept,
In quiet paths, our hearts have stepped.

Veiled Yearnings

Behind the curtains of the night,
Lies a flame that burns so bright.
In shadows deep, desires hide,
A longing that we cannot fight.

Eyes meet in a fleeting glance,
A silent plea for one more chance.
In every touch, a whispered plea,
For love to set our spirits free.

The quiet ache within the chest,
A secret hope that we're blessed.
In dreams we find our sweet release,
Yearnings told with tender peace.

Intimate Harmonies

Soft melodies in twilight's gleam,
We weave together like a dream.
Notes of love, so pure and true,
In every chord, a vow renewed.

Fingers dance on ivory keys,
Echoes of our hearts' decrees.
Harmony in every beat,
A symphony where souls do meet.

In the still of night's embrace,
We find our own secluded space.
Love's duet, forever plays,
In intimate harmonies, our hearts stay.

Subtle Serenades

In the quiet of the dawn,
A song of love is gently drawn.
With every note, a story told,
In subtle serenades of old.

Gentle breezes carry tunes,
Underneath the watching moon.
Lyrics whispered on the wind,
Love's sweet serenade begins.

In moments pure and hearts aligned,
A melody so softly twined.
Subtle as a lover's kiss,
In serenades, we find our bliss.

Echoes of Emotions

In caverns deep where shadows play,
Emotions find their voice,
Reflected hues of night and day,
In whispers they rejoice.

A symphony of silent tears,
Resounds in hearts concealed,
Through laughter's light or sorrow's fears,
True feelings are revealed.

The echoes stretch through time and space,
Each pulse a tender vestige,
Of moments lost or love's embrace,
An everlasting message.

Beneath the Breaths

Beneath the breaths of morning light,
The world unfurls anew,
Each sigh, a canvas painted bright,
With whispers soft and true.

Inhale the scent of dreams unfurled,
Exhale the thoughts unspoken,
Between the threads of waking world,
Lie promises unbroken.

In every pause, a silent cry,
Unseen, yet vibrant, glowing,
Beneath our breaths, the heartbeats lie,
In secret rhythms flowing.

Silent Sentiments

In silence, sentiments arise,
Unseen, yet deeply felt,
Through quiet glances, longing sighs,
In shadows, hearts do melt.

No need for words, the soul will speak,
In languages untold,
A tender touch, a tear's soft streak,
Emotions pure and bold.

The silent tides of inner seas,
In murmurs, gently flow,
Unveiling truths with subtle ease,
In hushed, profound echo.

Veins of Verity

Through veins of verity, life streams,
With truths both harsh and tender,
Each pulse, a testament to dreams,
In clarity and splendor.

No guise can shield the honest light,
That courses through our being,
Within the dark or in the bright,
The essence we are seeing.

In every heartbeat, truth is found,
In veins where life is flowing,
A constant rhythm, pure and sound,
The seeds of verity sowing.

Softly Spoken

In whispers, breezes pass the trees,
A secret dance in summer's ease.
Under the moon, the shadows play,
A symphony in twilight's sway.

Petals fall like gentle words,
Landing softly, barely heard.
Stars emerge in velvet night,
Whispering dreams in silent light.

The creeks and brooks begin to hum,
Weaving tales of things to come.
Beneath the earth, a heart beats slow,
Tales of time in murmurs flow.

Masked Cadences

Behind the veil, a rhythm hides,
Echoes draped in moonlit tides.
A masquerade of night proceeds,
Waltzing between the trembling reeds.

Disguised in shadows, music plays,
A dance of dreams through foggy haze.
Phantom echoes in the night,
Unseen hands conduct the light.

Curtains drawn, the masks still linger,
A hidden tune on every finger.
In the hush, a melody,
Whispers cloaked in mystery.

Pulse of Silence

In the void, a heartbeat drums,
Silent as the past becomes.
Stillness hums, a quiet storm,
Echoes of a life long worn.

Midnight's whispers softly tread,
Threads of stories left unsaid.
In spaces where no sound resides,
The pulse of silence gently guides.

Breath of night, caress the dawn,
In the calm, a spirit's drawn.
Moments fleeting, shadows trace,
The silent pulse, a steady pace.

Resonant Yearning

Deep within, the heart does long,
A resonant, unspoken song.
Through the echoes, yearning swells,
In every silence, it compels.

Wistful winds that sweep the plains,
Carry whispers, soft refrains.
Eyes that search the sky above,
For distant stars, for lost love.

Eternal quest, relentless pull,
In shadows, dreams remain full.
The heart's own voice, in silence heard,
A resonant, unending word.

Silent Devotion

In the hush of moonlit night,
Whispers of the heart take flight,
Stars above in spectral show,
Tidings of a love unknown.

Gentle winds through trees do sigh,
Echoes of a lullaby,
Souls entwined by fate's decree,
Silent vows of secrecy.

In each breath a soft caress,
Words unspoken yet confess,
Eyes that trace a timeless bond,
Depth of love in shadows spawned.

Pledges made in quiet's reign,
Threaded through both joy and pain,
Devotion pure as morning dew,
Eternal as the sky is blue.

With Every Pulse

Beneath the sky, so vast and wide,
Hearts beat strong with rhythmic pride,
Life within each second flows,
With every pulse, a story grows.

In moments brief but deeply felt,
Emotions rise, then softly melt,
Love's pure essence, fierce and bright,
In the daytime, in the night.

With every beat, a promise lives,
Echoes of the love it gives,
Bound by threads unseen but true,
In each heartbeat, I find you.

Life's symphony, so wild, sublime,
Marks our journey through the time,
With every pulse, we're drawn near,
In our love, we persevere.

Gentle Embrace

Morning breaks with golden hue,
Whispers dawn, a love anew,
In the quiet, soft and slow,
Gentle Embrace, hearts aglow.

Breezes weave through open fields,
Bringing solace, time reveals,
Every touch, a tender grace,
Sweetness found in soft embrace.

In twilight's glow, our spirits kiss,
Moments steeped in purest bliss,
Near or far, no space divides,
In your arms, my heart resides.

Through the storm and through the calm,
Love's soft touch, a healing balm,
In this dance of time and space,
Find me in our gentle embrace.

Love's Gentle Call

In the silence of the dawn,
When the night begins to yawn,
Love's soft murmur, tender, small,
Guides us with its gentle call.

Whispers in the evening breeze,
Comfort found with graceful ease,
Every sigh, a secret shared,
Souls like ours, so unprepared.

In the shadows, truth reveals,
Magic in the way it feels,
Holding close, our hearts enthrall,
Mesmerized by love's gentle call.

Moonlight dances on your face,
Love's enchantment, fleeting grace,
In the quiet night, we fall,
Bound forever by love's call.

Thoughtful Refrains

In the silence of the night, stars softly gleam
Whispers of wisdom in a wistful dream
Moonlight dances on a tranquil stream
Reflections of life, in a peaceful theme

Wandering thoughts, like leaves the fall
Memories echo down a timeless hall
Within the quiet, a distant call
To heed the heart, beyond the wall

Time flows gently, in a silent sweep
Secrets hidden in the depths they keep
Moments savored, in the dreams we reap
Thoughts entwined, in a slumber deep

Echoing Emotions

Heartfelt whispers on the breeze so light
Carrying dreams through the silent night
In the hush of dawn, new hopes ignite
Feelings linger, in the softest twilight

Tides of sorrow, waves of joy they blend
Echoing emotions that never end
Through life's journey, every bend
Love's refrain, a constant friend

Beneath the shadows, sunlight's grace
Emotions dance in a tender trace
In every heartbeat, a warm embrace
Echoes of life, find their place

Beneath the Surface

Underneath the surface, shadows play
Hidden realms where secret thoughts sway
Veins of mystery weave the night and day
In the silence, subtle whispers stay

Beneath the mask, true feelings lie
Ocean depths, where dreams never die
In the whispers of the wind, they sigh
Undercurrents where realities vie

In the quiet depths, our souls align
Subtle truths, in shadows benign
Lost in the riddle of the grand design
Beneath the surface, the stars still shine

Soul's Subtle Beat

In the quiet heart, a rhythm starts
Subtle whispers that gentle hearts impart
Beating softly in the tenderest parts
Carrying echoes from time's ancient arts

Through the chaos, a melody so sweet
In silence profound, the soul's subtle beat
Like a tender touch, profound yet discreet
Guiding steps on life's uncertain street

In every breath, a whisper's grace
Anchoring rhythms in a hasty pace
Soul's melody, a serene embrace
Echoing through time, a lasting trace

Rumors of the Heart

Whispers float in moonlit air,
Secrets told without a care,
Echoes dance in shadowed glen,
Rumors of the heart, again.

Tender notes on evening breeze,
Softly swaying 'neath the trees,
Silent vows, unspoken dreams,
In twilight's gentle gleams.

Eyes that meet in hidden glance,
Stories shared in silent trance,
Mysteries that love imparts,
Whispers are the heart's own arts.

Yearning looks and fleeting sighs,
Tangled fates and unknown ties,
In the night where wishes dart,
Rumors stir within the heart.

Soft Serenades

Melodies in twilight's hush,
Whispers soft, like gentle brush,
Notes that sway on night's cool air,
Soft serenades everywhere.

Stars that twinkle in the sky,
To the songs they do reply,
Moonbeams dance on ocean's wave,
To the tunes that night winds gave.

Hearts then flutter to the beat,
In the night's embrace, they meet,
Lovers' words in sweet accord,
Soft serenades they have poured.

In the glow of soft moonlight,
Dreams take flight in sheer delight,
Every touch, a tender chord,
Soft serenades to be adored.

Subtle Yearnings

Hidden glances, fleeting sigh,
In the silence, whispers fly,
Questions buried deep within,
Subtle yearnings, they begin.

Eyes that speak with voiceless grace,
Telling secrets, face to face,
Moments caught in frozen time,
Yearnings dance in silent rhyme.

Dreams that linger, softly stay,
Faint desires, night and day,
In the stillness, hearts reveal,
Yearnings that they can't conceal.

Gentle signals, wordless plea,
In the quiet, souls agree,
Threads of longing, deftly spin,
Subtle yearnings, deep within.

Silent Rhapsodies

Symphonies in silence speak,
Harmony, the sound they seek,
Notes that glide on feathered wings,
Silent rhapsodies love sings.

Moonlit nights and starry skies,
Silent music softly ties,
Whispers of a heart's delight,
Rhapsodies in quiet light.

Every breath, a gentle sound,
In the stillness, love is found,
Quiet ballets, hearts in flight,
Silent songs throughout the night.

In the hush, emotions blend,
Through the calm, the souls ascend,
Wordless tunes that time suspends,
Silent rhapsodies transcend.

Whispers of Passion

In the silence of twilight's embrace,
Soft murmurs weave through the air,
Hearts ignite in a celestial space,
Two souls entwined, tender and rare.

The stars above, witnesses to love,
Unseen, yet fervent, they flare,
Each whisper soft, a gentle shove,
Toward dreams they silently share.

Moonlight dances on skin like lace,
Breathes life to the night so bare,
In a sacred, secret place,
Eternal whispers declare.

Eyes speak with a fervent gleam,
In silence, their stories share,
Held in passion's vivid dream,
In whispers beyond compare.

The night yields to dawn's gentle kiss,
Silent vows now bright and fair,
Whispers of passion persist,
In the morning's tender care.

Vein-Born Affections

Through veins, the passion courses swift,
An unspoken, fervent lore,
In every heartbeat, hearts uplift,
Two beings longing for more.

Crimson rivers sing in delight,
With each pulse, a tale reborn,
Affections deep, pure and bright,
In every vein, love adorning.

Every touch, a spark ignites,
A warmth spreading through the core,
Vein-born affections take flight,
In endless, hidden rapport.

Beneath the skin, secrets flow,
Life's tender symphony roars,
In each embrace, their love shows,
Within veins, emotions pour.

Connected by invisible strings,
In silent harmony soar,
Vein-born affections bring,
Two hearts closer, evermore.

Pulsing Emotions

Against the rhythm of time's beat,
Emotions pulse, vast and clear,
In moments where two hearts meet,
A symphony for hearts to hear.

Each throb, a story in disguise,
Of love, of loss, and hope revered,
Pulsing emotions under night skies,
Where silent whispers are steered.

Through veins, feelings intertwine,
A tapestry woven sheer,
Pulsing emotions align,
Creating bonds, tender and dear.

In every sigh, in every glance,
Unseen yet profoundly near,
Pulsing emotions enhance,
The language of love sincere.

As dawn creeps with golden hues,
Emotions pulse without fear,
In the morning's gentle blues,
Their silent vows ring clear.

Intimate Whispers

In the stillness, breaths do blend,
With whispers soft, they appear,
Their silent language, hearts mend,
Intimate whispers they bear.

A tender glance, words unspoken,
With gentle whispers they steer,
Through the night, a bond unbroken,
Intimate whispers sincere.

In moon's glow, secrets unfold,
Stories and dreams they endear,
In the whispers, love so bold,
Lingering with each tear.

Eyes locked in a silent song,
Voice tender, calm, and clear,
Every whisper, pure and strong,
Intimate whispers they revere.

As morning light breaks the night,
Whispers fade, yet still near,
In the day's warmth and light,
Their love whispers without fear.

Sotto Voce Feelings

In twilight's soft whisper, emotions arise,
Veiled in moon's glow, beneath starlit skies.
Quiet as shadows, they drift and they dance,
Echoes of dreams in a moonlit trance.

Heartbeats like whispers, fragile and kind,
Secrets unspoken, to night they are blind.
Threads of connection, tender, unseen,
Woven like lace in a quiet scene.

Mutual silence, more eloquent than words,
Like melodies played by unseen birds.
An intimate symphony begins to unfold,
Stories in murmurs, softly retold.

The world fades away, lost in the hush,
Moments eternal, no need to rush.
Eyes meeting eyes, the silence profound,
In sotto voce, true love is found.

Soulful Echoes

Through valleys of time, memories flow,
Echoes of laughter, whispers of woe.
Ghostly vestiges of days gone by,
In corridors of spirit, they softly lie.

Each echo a veiling of souls intertwined,
Carried like leaves by the whispering wind.
Songs of the ancients, heartfelt and pure,
In twilight's embrace, their truths endure.

Beneath the veneer of tangible reality,
Reside echoes of timeless vulnerability.
Lingering phrases, once boldly spoken,
Now faint whispers of hearts once broken.

Silent reflections in the still of the night,
Flickers of past moments bathed in light.
Soulful echoes in the wind gently sway,
Ever-present reminders by night and by day.

Flickers of Affection

In the briefest glance, affection ignites,
A silent spark in the dimmest of lights.
Moments ephemeral, yet deeply profound,
In the flicker of love, we're beautifully bound.

Whispered gestures, tender and sweet,
Passion expressed in the spaces we meet.
A brush of the hand, a knowing smile,
Flickers of affection make life worthwhile.

Hearts bound by threads, delicate and thin,
In the light of love, forever we'll spin.
A symphony of emotions in every glance,
Celebrating love in each fleeting chance.

In shadow and light, our spirits entwine,
In the dance of affection, forever align.
With each small flicker, our souls connect,
Illuminating paths that we least expect.

Delicate Cadences

Gentle rhythms of life softly unfold,
Melodies in silence, stories gently told.
Delicate cadences in the hush of the night,
Ballet of whispers in twilight light.

Soft as a feather, time's footsteps tread,
Caressing the lines where dreams are fed.
Moments that linger, tender as dawn,
In delicate cadences, love moves on.

In the space between words, a song lies,
Eloquent silence under moonlit skies.
Each note a caress, each pause a sigh,
Love's delicate cadences, soaring high.

With every heartbeat, a melody weaves,
Through the tapestry of nights and eves.
In life's orchestra, our hearts take their stance,
Lost in delicate cadences, our souls dance.

Emotion's Echo

In twilight's gentle sighs,
Where whispers softly blend,
A symphony of skies,
Begins where shadows end.

The echoes linger near,
A heartstring's quiet plea,
In sorrow's silent tear,
A song for you and me.

Beneath the moon's embrace,
Where dreams and feelings flow,
A tender, sacred space,
Where secret gardens grow.

Unveiled by night's caress,
The stars in tandem gleam,
In echoes of distress,
Our hearts begin to dream.

Each emotion finds its voice,
A delicate refrain,
In moments we rejoice,
And heal the quiet pain.

Depths of Affection

In oceans deep and wide,
Where love's pure currents sweep,
Affection's gentle tide,
Embraces hearts that leap.

A whisper on the breeze,
A tender touch of grace,
In passion's warm reprise,
We find our sacred place.

The depths conceal our truth,
In shadows soft and mild,
A love that breeds in youth,
And grows, unchained, and wild.

With every anchor cast,
Our souls are intertwined,
In present, future, past,
Affection's ties we find.

Beyond the bounds of speech,
Where silence speaks our name,
In depths of love, we reach,
Eternal and the same.

Tender Undertones

Beneath the surface lies,
A symphony unseen,
Where tender undertones,
Compose a love serene.

In every fleeting glance,
And every subtle touch,
Our hearts begin to dance,
In cadence, oh so much.

A whisper in the night,
A breath against the skin,
In undertones of light,
Our secret selves begin.

Through life's delightful hues,
And in its darkest shade,
Our bond forever true,
In tender tones is made.

Unfolding like a dream,
Our love's soft melody,
A quiet, gentle theme,
That sings eternally.

Rhythms of the Heart

In rhythms soft and sweet,
Where pulses beat as one,
Our hearts in love both meet,
Beneath the setting sun.

A dance that knows no end,
A melody so pure,
In rhythms hearts defend,
A beat that will endure.

Through every rise and fall,
In every silent pause,
We answer love's soft call,
Without a need for cause.

The tempo of our days,
In sync with gentle grace,
In heartbeats love conveys,
A time and tender place.

Together we shall waltz,
Through life's expansive chart,
In rhythms true, no faults,
The music of the heart.

Gentle Whispers

In the silence of the night,
Soft whispers drift and weave,
Carrying dreams on starlit breezes,
To hearts that dare believe.

Moonlight paints the canvas,
Of secrets softly told,
As shadows dance in twilight's rim,
And mysteries unfold.

Leaves rustle in the quiet,
A lullaby so sweet,
Promising with each breath taken,
A love that's meant to meet.

The wind caresses gently,
Lines written in the air,
A story pieced together,
Without a hint of care.

In these gentle whispers,
A symphony takes flight,
Comfort for the weary soul,
Guiding through the night.

Resonant Pulses

Beneath the quiet surface,
A heartbeat strong and true,
Echoes in the hollow places,
Waves that gently strew.

The rhythm of the ages,
In pulses deep and grand,
Draws the fabric of existence,
With an unseen hand.

Songs of ancient forest,
And whispers of the sea,
Merge into a single note,
Of fated harmony.

In every beat that lingers,
Resides a cosmic tune,
Binding hearts and souls alike,
In resonant commune.

So listen to the cadence,
Of life that never ceases,
A timeless, boundless melody,
Where every moment pleases.

Inner Symphony

Within the heart's vast chamber,
A symphony does play,
Notes of joy and sorrow,
That ebb and flow each day.

From whispers soft and tender,
To crescendos bold and bright,
A dance of inner melodies,
That shine in darkest night.

Emotions are the players,
In this endless, silent score,
Crafting tales of love and loss,
Through windows and through doors.

Each beat a revelation,
Each pause a breath of peace,
Together they compose a life,
Where worries find release.

So heed your inner symphony,
Its music raw and true,
For in its timeless echoes,
Your soul's own light will renew.

Unvoiced Hopes

In the quiet of the morning,
Hopes rise with the dawn,
Unvoiced yet ever present,
To light where dreams are drawn.

A wish that's barely whispered,
On lips that softly part,
Carries the weight of endless skies,
Within a beating heart.

An ember softly glowing,
In shadows deep and dark,
Guides the weary wanderer,
To find a loving spark.

Though words may never utter,
The hopes one dares to dream,
They flow within like rivers,
A silent, sacred stream.

So tend to these unvoiced hopes,
With every breath you take,
For in their tender nurturing,
A new dawn you awake.

Emotional Cadence

In the rhythm of the heart, a song so pure,
Where feelings dance and bravely endure.
A cadence soft, with whispers clear,
Emotions rise and fall, drawing us near.

Sorrows mingle with the notes of joy,
Each beat a story, neither girl nor boy.
For in this symphony, all voices blend,
A melody of hearts, no end to mend.

Hope and pain entwine like lovers lost,
In shadows cast by life's eternal cost.
Yet light breaks through with every strum,
In rhythmic echoes, where dreams come.

A silent tear may join the chorus vast,
Memories forging ties that surely last.
Within each measure, a spirit free,
Emotional cadence, our endless plea.

Subtle Affections

In gentle sighs and fleeting glance,
Subtle affections weave their dance.
Unspoken words that softly glow,
In twilight's tender, quiet show.

A touch so brief, yet deeply felt,
Where hearts in secret whispers melt.
Each smile a promise, shy and sweet,
A silent love where spirits meet.

The morning dew on petals fine,
Reflects the grace of love's design.
Invisible, yet plain to see,
This bond, delicate and free.

Through passing days and starlit skies,
A love that needs no grand disguise.
In every look, a story spins,
Subtle affections, where love begins.

Touched by Tenderness

A simple touch can heal the soul,
In moments when we're not quite whole.
For tenderness, a balm so rare,
In hearts entwined, beyond compare.

A whispered word, a gentle hand,
In these, we come to understand.
That even in the darkest night,
Tenderness brings forth the light.

A comfort found in quiet grace,
A tender kiss, a soft embrace.
In every gesture, love is known,
These tender moments, all our own.

When sorrow strikes and shadows fall,
It's tenderness that answers call.
A love that lives in softest touch,
For in this warmth, we feel so much.

Whispers in the Dark

In the quiet of the night's embrace,
Whispers in the dark find their place.
Secrets shared in shadows deep,
Dreams unfold as we gently sleep.

Voices low, like muted breeze,
Stories told with utmost ease.
In night's soft cloak, we find our mark,
Conniving whispers in the dark.

Stars above, in silent gleam,
Witness whispers of our dream.
A world revealed, when lights depart,
Hidden whispers from the heart.

In the stillness, fears are quelled,
Truths emerge, long withheld.
In shadows, confidences spark,
Soulful whispers in the dark.

Faint Melodies

In twilight's gentle embrace,
Soft notes begin to sing.
A lullaby of evening grace,
Where shadows and dreams take wing.

Stars twinkle a silent song,
Their light a subtle guide.
Through the night so vast and long,
With whispers that can't hide.

The moon's a harp in the sky,
Plucking tunes so fine.
Melodies that drift and sigh,
In a pattern, divine.

Amidst the hush of the trees,
A symphony unfolds.
Carried on the quiet breeze,
In mysteries untold.

As dawn approaches slow,
Those faint notes gently fade.
A promise in their glow,
In morning's light remade.

Intimacy and Echoes

In the quiet of a heartbeat,
Love's whispers softly tread.
Each echoing retreat,
A promise softly said.

Hands that clasp in night,
Fingers weave in trust.
The world's vast, out of sight,
Moments timeless, just.

Eyes that speak in silence,
A language all their own.
In every breath, compliance,
Together, never alone.

The echoes softly linger,
Within the soul's deep well.
Each touch, a gentle singer,
In the spaces where we dwell.

As voices fade to longing,
And memories softly weave.
In love's quiet belonging,
Heart to heart, we cleave.

Silent Harmonies

The river flows in murmurs low,
A symphony unseen.
Its current crafts a gentle show,
In the spaces between.

Leaves rustle a quiet tune,
In the forest deep.
Their song a whispered monsoon,
Lulling the earth to sleep.

Mountains hum a secret hymn,
Standing tall and grand.
Their melodies pure and trim,
Woven by nature's hand.

Waves brush the shore in time,
A rhythm unconfined.
In each crest a silent rhyme,
To the cosmos aligned.

And in the heart of stillness,
A harmony takes flight.
Silent, yet profound fullness,
In the tranquil night.

Whispers of the Soul

In the stillness of the night,
A voice within speaks clear.
Its whispers soft, a gentle light,
Cast upon the ear.

Dreams arise like tender blooms,
In the garden of the mind.
Their fragrance fills the silent rooms,
A solace we can find.

Memories dance with subtle grace,
In the chambers of the heart.
Each moment leaves a sacred trace,
Of the soul's true art.

Through life's quiet passages,
Wisdom gently flows.
Unseen, yet it presages,
The path our spirit knows.

When morning breaks with golden hue,
Those whispers still remain.
A silent guide, forever true,
Through joy, through love, through pain.

Radiant Softness

In the hush of dawn's embrace,
Whispers of the morning's grace,
Sunlight through the trees does weave,
Golden threads of light reprieve.

Petals bloom with tender sigh,
Underneath the expansive sky,
Each dewdrop holds a secret bright,
A dance of diamonds in soft light.

Meadows hum a silent song,
To the day where hearts belong,
Nature's breath in stillness laid,
Radiant softness, serenade.

Breeze caresses with gentle hand,
Across the quiet, sleeping land,
Whispering tales of growth anew,
In every shade and muted hue.

Evening falls with velvet kiss,
Wrapping all in twilight's bliss,
Stars alight in silent cheer,
Embodying the softness, near.

Soul Murmurs

In whispers low, the soul does speak,
In quiet tones, the heart does seek,
A tapestry of thoughts, so rare,
Woven in the midnight air.

Echoes of the past remain,
In the soft, unending rain,
Secrets of the stars align,
In the silent, vast divine.

Every breath, a furtive plea,
In the depths of you and me,
Conversations without sound,
In the murmurs, we are found.

Moonlight paints the silent night,
Revealing all that's hidden, bright,
Soul to soul, we gently share,
The whispers of the love we wear.

In the calm of twilight's gleam,
We find the echoes of our dream,
Soul murmurs, soft and true,
In the quiet, me and you.

Tender Reverberations

Echoes in the heart persist,
In the spaces where we kissed,
Soft reverberations play,
In the gentle light of day.

Memories in shadows cast,
Whispers of a love that lasts,
Tender tones of yesteryears,
Resonate through joyful tears.

Like a song in soft reprise,
Sung beneath the endless skies,
Every note a cherished thread,
Woven where our hearts were led.

Crystals in the moonlight dance,
Radiant in love's expanse,
Mirrored in our quiet gaze,
Tender in these fleeting days.

In the stillness, feel it there,
Echoes ringing in the air,
Tender reverberations blend,
In the silence, we transcend.

Luminous Quiet

In the heart of twilight's glow,
Where the quiet rivers flow,
Peace descends like whispered prayer,
Calming breath in luminous air.

Stars awaken, soft and bright,
Guardians of the tranquil night,
In the silence, dreams take flight,
Bathed in soft, ethereal light.

Whispers of the night unfold,
Stories of the ancients told,
In the stillness, truth is found,
In the glow, the world is drowned.

Candles flicker, shadows play,
In the quiet, hearts can sway,
Moments stretch in boundless grace,
Light illuminates each trace.

In this sacred, muted trance,
Every breath an endless dance,
Luminous and quiet reign,
In the silence, we remain.

Veiled Pulses

In the shadowed dance of night,
Whispers blend with beams of light.
Hearts concealed by layers dense,
Beat in twilight's soft pretense.

Stars embark on secret quests,
Guiding dreams in moonlit nests.
Hidden rhythms find their grace,
In the vast, uncharted space.

Curtains drawn by zephyr's hand,
Unveil the mystic, boundless land.
Echoes wrap the quiet air,
In the realms beyond compare.

Veiled are the pulses deep inside,
Where dark and light in balance ride.
Tales unseen, yet felt profound,
In the echoes of heart's ground.

Twilight whispers in disguise,
Hidden truths and silent ties.
Veils withdraw, and pulses bloom,
In the silence, love's perfume.

Underneath the Silence

Where the quiet shadows lie,
Words unsaid still mystify.
Beneath the hush of night's embrace,
Whispers dwell in sacred space.

Moonlight's fingers trace the air,
Secrets soft and visions rare.
Unheard murmurs gently stream,
Through the silence, like a dream.

In the stillness, echoes yearn,
For the light of hearts to burn.
Unseen currents, strong and pure,
Travel through the silence, sure.

Stars reflect the silent plea,
In their gaze, infinity.
Underneath the tranquil sky,
Emotions drift, and spirits fly.

Hushed, the world bespeaks its tales,
Through the silence, calm prevails.
Hidden depths reveal their might,
In the quiet, hearts unite.

Gentle Reverberations

Softly through the evening's veil,
Echoes drift on winds so frail.
Whispers sway in tender waves,
In the quiet, courage braves.

Sunset's touch with hues does weave,
Hope in every leaf and eve.
Gentle sounds of twilight's fall,
Answer to the heart's soft call.

Lilting birds with songs so light,
Reverberate through coming night.
Each note hangs, a tender prayer,
Floating on the tranquil air.

Breezes carry secrets long,
In their strains, a silent song.
Underneath the twilight's hand,
Gentle whispers grace the land.

Subtle echoes hint and play,
In the twilight's soft display.
Every gentle reverberation,
Speaks of love's sincere creation.

Unheard Vows

Beneath the stars, in still retreat,
Heartfelt vows go on repeat.
Silence hears the promises,
Whispered soft through night's abyss.

Gazes share unspoken dreams,
In the quiet, love redeems.
Hands entwine with tender grace,
Bond eternal, time can't erase.

Moonlight seals the silent pact,
Feelings pure, with truth intact.
Every glance, a wordless plea,
Bound in perpetuity.

Night-time holds the sacred trust,
In its calm, the vows adjust.
Unheard, yet profoundly known,
In their depth, the love has grown.

Stars align and bless the night,
Witness to the vows so bright.
Love unspoken, yet avowed,
In the silence, hearts are proud.

Veiled Vows

In twilight's glow our secrets breathe,
Veiled in whispers, shadows wreathe.
Promises in darkness sown,
Where only moonlit truths are known.

Beneath the stars, we weave our plight,
Hidden from the piercing sight.
Hearts entangled, yet apart,
Silent vows that stir the heart.

The night enfolds our whispered dreams,
In shadows' dance, our fate redeems.
Eyes that glisten with untold fears,
In twilight's hush, our love adheres.

Vows unseen by morning's ray,
In moon's embrace they softly lay.
Ephemeral, yet deeply bound,
In veiled vows, our hearts are found.

The dawn will break, reveal the day,
But twilight vows in heart will stay.
The night, our silent guardian,
Of veiled vows that forever stand.

Sentimental Threads

In silken strands, our memories lie,
Woven deep beneath the cry.
Of time that whispers, forever bound,
In sentimental threads we're found.

Each thread a tale of joy and woe,
In tapestry, our lives bestow.
Patterns form with love and pain,
Intricate, in beauty's reign.

The loom of life, its twists and turns,
In every thread, a lesson earns.
We stitch together night and day,
In sentimental threads, we stay.

Colors bright and shadows stark,
In cloth of life, they leave their mark.
Intertwined, our stories told,
In threads of sentiment, bold.

In every weave, a piece of heart,
Together stitched, we'll never part.
In seamless bond of joy and dread,
Our love is in these threads beheld.

Faint Heartbeats

Within the quiet of the night,
Faint heartbeats whisper out of sight.
Echoes of a love so pure,
In silence, hearts forever sure.

Beneath the stars, our pulses blend,
In rhythm, soaring without end.
Tender murmurs, soft as mist,
In faint heartbeats, we're gently kissed.

The nightingale's song, a fleeting grace,
Yet in our hearts it finds its place.
For love's sweet hum within us lies,
In every beat, a sweet reprise.

Quiet moments, souls entwined,
In every heartbeat, love defined.
Together bound, no need for words,
In silence, our true selves are heard.

Faint heartbeats, a symphony,
In softest notes, our love set free.
Unseen, yet always felt within,
Our heartbeats' song will never dim.

Silent Symphonies

A silent symphony unfolds,
In twilight hush, it softly holds.
The melodies of stars above,
A cosmic tune of endless love.

Night's orchestra, in shadows play,
A symphony of dark and day.
Without a note, its beauty streams,
In silence, music of our dreams.

Soft whispers of the autumn breeze,
In symphonies that never cease.
The rustling leaves, a gentle song,
In silent notes, where hearts belong.

Moonlight's glow, the silver hue,
Composes tunes for me and you.
In silent waltz, across the skies,
A symphony that never lies.

Silent symphonies that bind,
Melodies within the mind.
Unheard by ears, but felt by heart,
In silent music, never part.

Breathless Sighs

In twilight's tender, soft embrace,
Two souls align in gentle grace.
Eyes flicker 'neath the velvet skies,
Unspoken love, breathless sighs.

Whispered secrets, moonlit night,
Hearts entwine, a hopeful plight.
Time stands still, no need for why,
Just the magic of that sigh.

Stars above begin to dance,
Lovers lost in sweet romance.
Every breath a silent cry,
Within each other's breathless sigh.

Moments fleeting, yet they stay,
In memories that never fray.
Captured in that whispered sky,
Love transcends with breathless sighs.

Hand in hand, the world is theirs,
Unseen threads, the night repairs.
Infinite in a lover's eye,
Endless echo, breathless sigh.

Heartstrings' Melody

A serenade within the breeze,
Love's sweet chime through ancient trees.
Echoes soft, both pure and free,
Playing heartstrings' melody.

Notes of life, a symphony,
Binding souls through harmony.
Chords of passion, strong and free,
Fused in heartstrings' melody.

Every beat, a story told,
Woven threads of love unfold.
Eternal song, a loving plea,
Bound in heartstrings' melody.

Gentle whispers, night's caress,
Rhythms of a love's finesse.
Harmony in you and me,
Pour from heartstrings' melody.

In the silence, music sways,
Gifts of love in waves convey.
Forevermore our hearts shall see,
Life's sweet heartstrings' melody.

Gentle Reverie

In dreams, a world of tender shade,
Where worries drift and fears do fade.
A fleeting realm of soft embrace,
A gentle reverie, our place.

Whispers float on tranquil streams,
Nightly tapestries of dreams.
Serene and calm, a sacred space,
Within this gentle reverie, peace.

Shadows blend with hues of light,
Painting visions through the night.
Heart and soul find soft release,
In realms of gentle reverie, love's peace.

Timeless moments, endless seas,
Life's pure essence, soul agrees.
Restful sighs in dreams, increase,
The gift of gentle reverie, ease.

Carried through the night's soft glow,
Waking, we shall always know,
Dreamt-of realms where all's set free,
A world of gentle reverie.

Subdued Echoes

In the quiet of the night,
Voices fade, subdued delight.
Memories whisper, soft and low,
Within the realm where echoes flow.

Shadows dance in moonlight's grace,
Unseen tears on a silent face.
Time's soft laps, the moments show,
Tales of love in subdued echo.

Ghostly touch of yesteryears,
Gentle brush of hopes and fears.
Heartbeats merge, a subtle blow,
Lost within the subdued echo.

Stars look down and quietly sigh,
Witness to each lover's cry.
Hopes that rise, then softly go,
Travel with the subdued echo.

When morning breaks and light returns,
Silent echoes fade and yearn.
Yet still, the heart will always know,
The song of love's subdued echo.

Heartstrings' Hum

In twilight's soft embrace, hearts gently hum,
Two souls entwined, a silent tune begun.
Whispers melt like dew beneath the sun,
In warmth of love, all doubts become undone.

Beyond horizons where the shadows cease,
We find a comfort, tender, quiet peace.
Echoes of dreams, from years long past to lease,
Accentuate a bond that will not cease.

Soft breath of night, composed with every touch,
A melody that says so very much.
In every heartbeat, feelings intertwine,
A symphony of love's unwritten line.

In silent moments, hearts in harmony,
Compose a timeless, tender symphony.
With every glance, a note of sweet decree,
A serenade, a gentle rhapsody.

Together in this quiet, we become,
The echo of our hearts, the soft, sweet hum.
Each verse a testament to love begun,
A melody that binds as we succumb.

Barely Spoken

Soft murmurs dance on lips that scarcely part,
In every word, a world, a tender art.
Emotions cloaked in whispers light and pure,
In silence shared, a solace to ensure.

Eyes lock in gentle rays, a silent song,
The space between, a place where love belongs.
No need for words when feelings overwhelm,
In quietude, love's whispers helm.

A breath, a glance, a fleeting smile conveys,
More than a thousand words in countless ways.
In stillness, find a love that softly stays,
Filling the gaps with unspoken praise.

Through quiet nights and dawns of muted gold,
In every pause, a story to be told.
A poem crafted, neither young nor old,
In the whispers, lives love uncontrolled.

Through unvoiced thoughts, emotions freely glide,
In silence, where our deepest feelings hide.
Barely spoken, yet firmly intertwined,
Our hearts converse, our souls coincided.

Understated Beat

Beneath the surface, silent rhythms trace,
An understated beat in every place.
Unsung melodies that softly grace,
The essence of a love that leaves no trace.

Gentle pulses, in the stillness found,
A subtle cadence, echoing around.
In every heart, a secret, silent sound,
That keeps our love forever tightly bound.

A rhythm that beneath the noise prevails,
Sublime and constant, like the moon's own trails.
An unassuming song through life's travails,
In quiet moments, love's true essence sails.

Within the calm, a heartbeat draws us near,
An understated beat we hold so dear.
Through whispered moments, nothing left unclear,
Love's quiet rhythm all we ever hear.

In silence, where the loudest feelings meet,
Find harmony with life's understated beat.
A pulse that carries us through incomplete,
Moments, till our love is whole and sweet.

Lingering Notes

In echoes left by gentle, fleeting touch,
Lingering notes remind us of so much.
A melody that floats within us still,
Resonates with every pause and thrill.

In halls of silence, echoes softly lie,
Reverberating dearly through the sky.
The notes remain, though time may swiftly fly,
A testament to love, we can't deny.

Each moment shared, a chorus of the soul,
Lingering notes that make the spirit whole.
As time moves on, they quietly unroll,
A song of memories where we console.

Soft strains of love now tiptoe through the air,
In every look, the tune is always there.
A harmony that binds us unaware,
In tender notes, our hearts will ever share.

Within these lingering notes, our love survives,
A melody that dances, leaps, and thrives.
In every silent space, it re-arrives,
A constant song through all our precious lives.

Breath of Love

Beneath the twilight's gentle glow,
A whisper danced among the trees.
The breath of love that softly flows,
Through night-time's tender, quiet breeze.

Soft murmurs trace the moonlit sky,
Where dreams are sown in fields of night.
Two hearts entwined, they climb so high,
In love's embrace, pure and bright.

Stars bear witness from above,
To secrets shared in silent gaze.
The breath of love, a tender glove,
Wraps around, in endless daze.

As dawn awakes with hues of gold,
Their souls remain forever bound.
The breath of love, a story told,
In whispers sung without a sound.

With every beat, with every sigh,
The breath of love, it gently rolls.
On winds of time, it soars on high,
Forever etched in timeless scrolls.

Veins of Sentiment

Through veins of sentiment, it flows,
A river deep of echoed dreams.
In hidden paths, where heartbeats glow,
Love's melody in silent streams.

The pulse of life, it softly hums,
In rhythm with our inner tide.
With every throb, emotion drums,
A symphony we cannot hide.

In veins of sentiment, we're twined,
With threads of joy and threads of pain.
A tapestry our hearts have lined,
In sunshine and in falling rain.

Emotions flow, a crimson sea,
Through channels carved by time's own hand.
In every heartbeat's silent plea,
We find the strength to understand.

The veins of sentiment will guide,
Through storm and calm, through night and day.
In every pulse, our souls confide,
That love and life will find their way.

Heartbeat Chronicles

Beneath the sky of endless blue,
Lies a tale within each beat.
The heartbeat chronicles, so true,
Of lives entwined, with joys replete.

In every pulse, a story's told,
Of moments shared, of dreams we've spun.
The chronicles in hearts of gold,
Found in the light of every sun.

Echoed whispers in the dark,
As stars unfold their silent lore.
The heartbeat chronicles do mark,
Our journey through each open door.

With every thud, with every sigh,
A testament to love's embrace.
The chronicles where truths do lie,
In hearts that time cannot erase.

The beat goes on, the stories blend,
In rhythm to the soul's own song.
The heartbeat chronicles, our friend,
Where we belong all our lives long.

Inward Whispers

In quiet moments, shadows play,
Where inward whispers softly sound.
The words our hearts can never say,
In silent streams, are gently bound.

A gentle nudge, a soft caress,
The inward whispers guide our way.
In labyrinths of tenderness,
They light the path through night and day.

With every breath, a secret shared,
In language only souls can speak.
The inward whispers, hearts prepared,
To find the strength that all hearts seek.

Through storms of life, through calm and peace,
The whispers hold us, ever near.
In their embrace, our worries cease,
For inward whispers banish fear.

The inward whispers softly weave,
A tapestry of love and light.
In every beat, in every sleeve,
They paint our dreams in colors bright.

Whispers of Silence

In the hush of night, shadows fall,
Whispers of silence, a soothing call,
Stars waltz in a quiet expanse,
Heartbeats join in a timeless dance.

Beneath the moon's soft, gentle ray,
Moments of peace gently sway,
Crickets sing a lullaby sweet,
Silence echoes, calm and complete.

Silent whispers in the air,
Dreams and wishes freely share,
Through the night, whispers flow,
In silence, secrets softly grow.

The world in stillness, so profound,
In silence, mystic truths are found,
Each whisper carries stories old,
In hushed tones, the night unfolds.

Night's embrace, a tranquil shroud,
In whispers of silence, beauty vowed,
Each breath a quiet, tender sigh,
Until morning greets the sky.

Quiet Beats

Softly hums the heart in peace,
In quiet beats, worries cease,
Life's rhythm in a gentle flow,
Moments pass, tender and slow.

In the silence, love is known,
Quiet beats, a secret tone,
Soft echoes in a calm retreat,
Where heart and soul quietly meet.

Through the stillness, time proceeds,
Quiet beats sow tranquil seeds,
A life in peace, a heart so light,
In quiet, whispers take flight.

Gentle breezes, calm and true,
Quiet beats, dreams pursue,
Harmony in silent breath,
In quiet, life transcends death.

Each beat a promise, pure and clear,
In quiet, melodies endear,
Harmony in every stride,
Quiet beats, hearts open wide.

Heartbeat of Love

In the hush, a heartbeat sounds,
In every pulse, love unbounds,
Quiet rhythms, soft and slow,
In beats of love, hearts bestow.

Through the night, a tender thrum,
In the heartbeat, love does hum,
A symphony in quiet blend,
In love's beat, hearts ascend.

Moments pass in silent grace,
Love's heartbeat, a warm embrace,
In every pulse, a promise grand,
Two hearts beat, hand in hand.

In silence, love finds its way,
Heartbeat's rhythm, night and day,
In each throb, love whispers true,
Every heartbeat, I need you.

Together in the midnight glow,
Love's heartbeat, softly flows,
In every beat, love's refrain,
Echoes sweetly, again and again.

Strings of the Heart

Strings of the heart, softly play,
In gentle whispers, night and day,
Melodies of love, sweet and pure,
In every note, truth endures.

In tender chords, emotions weave,
Strings of the heart, never deceive,
Harmony in every thread,
Where hearts connect, softly led.

A symphony within unfolds,
Strings of the heart, love upholds,
Every string a story tells,
In the heart, magic dwells.

Through the quiet, strings resound,
A love in music, deeply found,
Each vibration, a gentle kiss,
In the heart, purest bliss.

Strings of the heart, play on true,
In every note, skies of blue,
Music of the soul so bright,
In heartstrings, love takes flight.

Pulse of the Unspoken

In silent shadows, whispers glide,
Echoes of words, where hearts confide.
Silent songs in twilight's hue,
A dance of thoughts, concealed from view.

In unvoiced realms, emotions stir,
An unspoken language, they concur.
Through glances shared, and smiles worn thin,
A universe of secrets, lies within.

Beneath the stillness, beats align,
A rhythm of the soul, so divine.
In every silence, a story waits,
For lips to part, and reveal fates.

Unheard melodies, timeless and pure,
In the quiet, their notes endure.
In the hush of night, dreams ignite,
Weaving silent verses into light.

Through silent winds, and unseen flight,
Words unsaid, set hearts alight.
In the pulse of the unspoken, truth lies,
A silent song that never dies.

Muted Beats

Beneath the world's chaotic grind,
Lies a rhythm, pure and kind.
Muted beats, a subtle sound,
In every heart, they can be found.

Echoes of life, where silence reigns,
In whispered words and gentle strains.
A symphony, both soft and fleet,
Hidden within each heartbeat.

In quiet moments, they come alive,
In silent rooms, they softly thrive.
A dance of time, in shadows cast,
A silent song, steadfast, vast.

Each muted beat, a hidden tale,
Of love found, and hearts that sail.
In the stillness, they confide,
In every breath, they quietly reside.

Through mists of calm, and tranquil air,
These beats unite us, unaware.
In the quiet, truth completes,
The tender hum of muted beats.

Graceful Murmurs

Graceful murmurs, softly sigh,
In the breeze, they flutter by.
Gentle whispers, like morning dew,
Touching souls with a quiet hue.

In the silence, voices blend,
Tales of wonder, without end.
In each breath, a song's release,
A melody of whispered peace.

They dance on air, in twilight's glow,
Invisible, yet hearts they know.
In shadows cast by moonlit streams,
They weave the fabric of our dreams.

Through quiet nights and tranquil days,
In silent hymns, their beauty stays.
In the calm, their echoes weave,
A tapestry of what we believe.

Graceful murmurs, timeless, pure,
In their silence, they endure.
A gentle choir, of life's refrain,
Whispered sweetly, in soft refrain.

Hidden Beats

In the quiet corners of the heart,
Lie hidden beats, a world apart.
Unseen rhythms, soft and slow,
Underneath life's vibrant flow.

They pulse in sync, with gentle pace,
A tender touch, an unseen grace.
In the stillness, they unfold,
A secret song, a tale untold.

In hushed tones, they softly play,
Guiding us through night and day.
The hidden beats, a silent guide,
In their cadence, we confide.

Each beat a note, in silent chords,
Flowing through us, without words.
In the space where shadows meet,
Lies the rhythm, soft and sweet.

In life's noisy, hurried sheet,
Listen close for hidden beats.
They write the music of the soul,
Connecting us, making us whole.

Soft Heartbeats

In the quiet dawn they rise,
Gentle rhythms, soft and wise,
Whispers of a secret song,
In the heart where dreams belong.

Tender pulses, softly speak,
Moments neither strong nor weak,
In the stillness, pure and bright,
They dance through the silent night.

Where the morning gently wakes,
And the world of dreams forsakes,
There they hum, those soft heartbeats,
Tracing paths where love repeats.

In the hush of evenings' grace,
When the stars begin to trace,
Softly, softly they shall play,
As the night turns dreams to day.

Through the life and through the heart,
They persist, a subtle art,
Beating on with quiet might,
Guiding us through day and night.

Passion's Silent Song

Hidden where the shadows lie,
Where the hearts can touch the sky,
Flows a song without a word,
Passion's secret, never heard.

In the glance of loving eyes,
It resides, though in disguise,
Echoes of a silent tune,
Beneath the soft and silver moon.

Lips may part, but not in speech,
Hearts reach out, and fingers teach,
In the quiet flame they burn,
Passion's song at every turn.

Words are hushed by love so pure,
Silent song will yet endure,
In each heartbeat softly found,
In the stillness, it resounds.

Where two souls in whispers meet,
There the song is hushed and sweet,
In the silence, love will wear,
Passion's song, forever there.

Timeless Pulses

Clock hands move, yet feelings still,
Through the ages, hearts will thrill,
Timeless pulses, never old,
Woven tales of love, retold.

In the shadows, in the light,
Every day and every night,
Pulses beat in steady rhyme,
Unchanged through the hands of time.

Eons pass; the world may fade,
Yet heart's rhythm, undismayed,
Carries forth the same sweet tune,
Underneath the changing moon.

Love is constant, love is true,
Beating steady, always new,
Through the chapters life will write,
Pulses guide us through the night.

Timeless tales with every beat,
In our hearts, they softly meet,
Binding past and future dreams,
In the pulse of love's sweet streams.

Unheard Whispers

In the silence, they are found,
Words that don't make any sound,
Unheard whispers in the air,
Secrets that two souls may share.

Breezes brush the leaves at dusk,
In the air, a fragrant musk,
Carrying the whispered trace,
Of the love no time can erase.

In the spaces, thin and still,
Echoes linger, soft and shrill,
Speechless thoughts between the lines,
Guided by unseen designs.

Voiceless tales in hearts reside,
Though unspoken, none can hide,
Each soft whisper, though unheard,
Holds the weight of every word.

In the quiet, feel them near,
Unheard whispers, calm and clear,
Words that float through time and space,
Finding solace in embrace.

Silent Symphony

In the hush of twilight's grace,
Whispers of a calm embrace,
Nature's tune, a silent sway,
Carries dreams of yesterdays.

Stars align in silent cheer,
Moonlight whispers, soft and clear,
Night's concerto, gently played,
In the glow of evening shade.

Winds hum through the twilight's veil,
Rustling leaves and distant hail,
Harmony in quiet streams,
Flowing into midnight dreams.

Silence speaks in muted tones,
Through the woods and over stones,
Melodies in stillness bloom,
Dancing in the quiet gloom.

Dew collects on petals frail,
Nature's secrets they unveil,
Silent symphony unfolds,
Stories that the nighttime holds.

Embracing Shadows

In the dusk where shadows play,
Secrets come from light's decay,
Whispered tales in muted shades,
Linger as the daylight fades.

Shadows drift in twilight's hand,
Painting dreams on silver sand,
In their dance, the night reveals,
Hidden paths and mystic deals.

Echoes stir where shadows meet,
Silent steps on moonlit street,
In their dance, a story spins,
Of the night and all its sins.

Darkness holds a soothing grace,
Embracing every hidden trace,
In the calm of shadowed night,
Eyes can see beyond the light.

From the depths of night they rise,
Shadows weave beneath the skies,
In their folds, a tender claim,
Embracing shadows, free of shame.

Echoes of Intimacy

In whispers soft, our secrets lie,
Between the stars and moonlit sky,
Echoes of our gentle touch,
Linger in the night so much.

Fingers trace where hearts align,
Silhouettes in evening's sign,
In the quiet, soft and slow,
Echoes of our closeness flow.

Breaths in sync, a mirrored beat,
Tender moments, twilight sweet,
In the dark, our voices blend,
Echoes that will never end.

Eyes that speak without a sound,
Silent vows in night abound,
Every glance a story told,
Echoes in the dark unfold.

In the silence, through the night,
Spirits dance in shared delight,
Echoes of our hearts set free,
In the night's intimacy.

Invisible Threads

Threads unseen, yet tightly wound,
Binding hearts in ties profound,
Silent links that form and weave,
Connections that we all believe.

Across the miles, through time's embrace,
Threads unseen, they interlace,
With each heartbeat, tugging near,
Invisible ties we hold dear.

Whispered thoughts on winds of night,
Threads that bridge the vastest plight,
In their weave, a strength unseen,
Yet so strong, and yet so keen.

Through the laughter, through the tears,
Threads unseen, they calm our fears,
Holding us when days are cold,
Invisible threads, a bond so bold.

In the dance of life's grand scheme,
Threads unseen fulfill the dream,
Binding souls in harmony,
Invisible yet plain to see.

Lingering Harmonies

In twilight's hush, a whisper sings,
Soft notes that drift on gentle wings.
Melodies from a star-lit tide,
In dreams they dwell, where shadows bide.

Across the fields where night unfolds,
A symphony in silence molds.
Each echo breathes a quiet plea,
Lingering harmonies setting free.

The breeze conveys a muted tune,
Resonance beneath the moon.
In stillness, every string does sound,
An orchestra in night profound.

Underneath the ancient sky,
The music lives, though notes pass by.
In every heart, a song remains,
A lasting chord in memory's veins.

When dawn awakes the world anew,
The harmonies dissolve from view.
But in the soul, their whispers stay,
Guiding light through each new day.

Felt Through Silence

In the hush where shadows curl,
A tale unfolds without a word.
Silent whispers softly twine,
In the heart, emotions stir.

Quiet moments hold their weight,
Unseen, but deeply felt within.
Every glance, a story weaves,
Silent truths beneath the din.

In the stillness of the night,
Echoes of unspoken dreams.
Through the silence, pulses life,
Filling space with shadowed beams.

No voice, yet voices fill the air,
In the silent, steady beat.
Connection felt without a sound,
In the stillness, hearts do meet.

As the quiet sun descends,
A world within begins to grow.
Felt through silence, love extends,
Quiet waters gently flow.

Submerged Sentiments

Beneath the waves, emotions sleep,
In ocean's heart, sentiments deep.
Currents weave a tale untold,
In quiet depths, mysteries unfold.

Submerged beneath the surface calm,
Whispers of a silent psalm.
Heartfelt echoes brush the soul,
In every swell, life's questions roll.

In twilight's blue, where silence sings,
Feelings float on hidden wings.
Uncharted depths within the mind,
In oceans vast, what love we find.

A silent plea in each soft wave,
Lessons of the heart engraved.
In quiet tides, so much is said,
In oceans deep, by feelings led.

As sunlight fades from ocean's crest,
Sentiments in peace do rest.
In every drop, a story lies,
Submerged beneath the boundless skies.

Delicate Echoes

A whispered word in twilight's glow,
A gentle breeze where echoes flow.
Soft refrains in evening's hush,
Delicate as morning's blush.

Each echo tells a tender tale,
In moonlight's soft, ethereal veil.
Silent songs of love and loss,
Within their cadence, futures cross.

The night holds whispers calm and still,
Each echo from the heart does spill.
In the quiet, feelings stir,
A timeless dance, a soft whim's murmur.

Reflections of a past once bright,
In echoes, still they shine so light.
Though faint, the memories remain,
In delicate echoes, love's refrain.

As dawn awakes with gentle breeze,
Echoes fade but leave their tease.
In hearts, they weave a golden thread,
Delicate echoes never dead.

9 789916 861882